You are C
Crowned by The King of Kings!

Chosen TO BE CROWNED

A 30-DAY JOURNEY TO RESTORE YOUR IDENTITY AND WORTH IN CHRIST!

"But you are a chosen people, a royal priesthood, a holy nation, God's special possession, that you may declare the praises of Him who called you out of darkness into His wonderful light."
1 Peter 2:9

JALICIA N. RICHARD

"Founder of Manners 2 Grace and Creator of A Femininity Care"

Published by Jalicia N. Richard
www.femininitycare.com

Printed in the United States of America.
ISBN: 978-1-7341252-2-1

THIS JOURNAL BELONGS TO

....

....

Dedication & Introduction

Hello there, my sister in Christ! I am beyond grateful that you are here! "***Chosen To Be Crowned:A 30-Day Journey to Restore Your Identity and Worth in Christ***" is dedicated to every woman and teen girl who has ever questioned her identity and worth, doubted her purpose, or felt unseen. May you be reminded: You are chosen, crowned, and loved beyond measure! Throughout this journey, I pray you find renewed strength and confidence in your identity, embracing the beautiful truth that you are uniquely created for a purpose. Together, let's discover the depth of God's love and the radiant worth He bestows upon each of us!

Throughout these next 30 days, you will embark on a powerful journey of rediscovering who you are in Christ. Each week is intentionally designed to guide you through a different aspect of your restoration journey. Whether it's embracing your uniqueness, shedding old habits, recognizing your worth, or affirming your divine identity, each day builds on the previous one. By taking the time to reflect, pray, and journal, you will discover deeper truths about who you are in Christ. This process is meant to empower you, reminding you that you are never alone and that God is always at work in your life, bringing healing and transformation. Embrace this journey with an open heart, and allow your spirit to flourish as you step into the fullness of what God has for you!

In **Week 1,** you will focus on reclaiming your identity in Christ and rediscovering who God says you are. In **Week 2**, you will embrace your royalty and worth as a daughter of the King. You will discover how to confidently wear your crown and recognize the value of your divine identity. Through reflections and activities, you will actively explore the beautiful truths about yourself and learn to walk in the authority and grace that God has bestowed upon you. Each day, you will be reminded of your unique worth and the incredible purpose you have as His beloved daughter. Get ready to embrace the life of royalty that is yours! In **Week 3,** you will experience healing and freedom as God begins to restore the broken places within you. You will actively seek His touch in your life and allow His love to mend your wounds. Then, in **Weeks 4 and 5,** you will step into your divine authority, embracing the crown that empowers you to reign and fulfill your God-given purpose. With confidence and grace, you will take on new challenges and pursue your calling, knowing that you are equipped and supported by Him every step of the way.

There was a time when I needed a reminder of who I am in Christ. Through God's grace and truth, I discovered that healing, deliverance, and

Restoration begins when I see myself the way He sees me. I pray that as you journey through these pages, you will experience that same transformation — one that brings peace, confidence, and renewal to your soul.

May the next 30 days remind you that you are "***Chosen To Be Crowned,***" handpicked by God to carry His glory and goodness wherever you go! Embrace each day with confidence, knowing you reflect His light and love. As you step into each moment, recognise that you are called to make an impact, spreading His grace and joy. Let your actions and words be a testament to His glory in your life, and remember that you are equipped to shine brightly in every circumstance. Walk boldly into your purpose, knowing that His divine hand guides you at every turn!

With Grace & Hugs,
Jalicia N. Richard

TABLE OF CONTENTS

WEEK 1

WEEK 2

TABLE OF CONTENTS

WEEK 3

WEEK 4

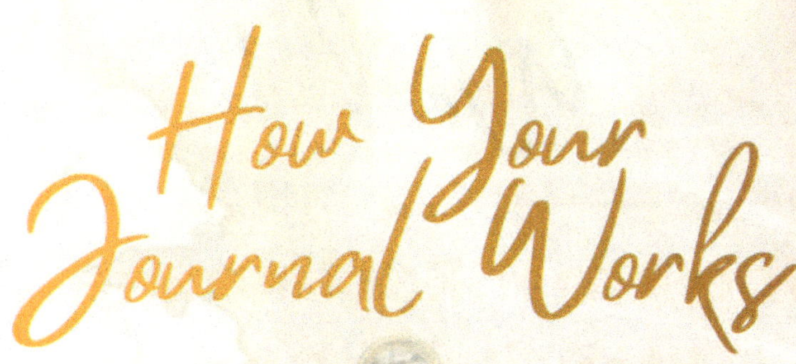

Your 30-day devotional journal consists of 5 different weeks:

Each day includes:

- A Scripture
- A Devotional Reading
- A Journal Prompt or Reflection
- A Declaration to Speak Over Yourself

Take your time with each day. Do not rush the process. Allow the Holy Spirit to reveal what He wants to heal, restore, and remind you of! You may choose to go through one devotional each morning to set the tone for your day or at night as a time of reflection. Write your thoughts, prayers, and revelations in the spaces provided, and revisit them often. This is your personal journey of transformation and each day, God will meet you right where you are!

Week 1:

Who Am I? Reclaiming My Identity in Christ!

Sis, before your name ever knew you, you were known by God. Before the world labelled you, compared you, or wounded you, He already called you *His.*

Week 1 is all about coming to who you truly are in Christ. For too long, many of us have lived beneath our true identity, shaped by what others said, what life has done, or what we have done to ourselves. But God wants to restore your name, your voice, and your confidence. He wants to remind you that your identity does not come from your past, your status, or your failures; it comes from *who you belong to.*

As you journey through these seven days, allow the Holy Spirit to rebuild your identity in His truth gently. Take a deep breath and open your heart. This is where restoration begins, with remembering who you are and **whose you are!**

This week's focus: An Identity Reminder!

Day 1:

"Chosen Before Creation"

"Even before He made the world, God loved us and chose us in Christ to be holy and without fault in His eyes." **Ephesians 1:4 (NLT)**

Sis, before the world was created, you were already on the mind of the Father. You were not an afterthought, an accident, or a mistake. When God chose you, you became His perfect decision, intentionally created and divinely selected. God handpicked you with purpose and care to carry His glory and reflect His love.

Even when the world tries to label you, remember that God has already named you: **Chosen!** This declaration means you are deeply loved and uniquely set apart. Whenever the world whispers lies, stand firm in God's truth: "God chooses me!" Let that truth empower you as you walk in confidence, knowing that you are valued and cherished beyond measure.

Prayer Declaration:
Dear God, thank you for choosing me even in a world that may try to label me. Even when I feel overlooked or unworthy, remind me you have already called me Yours.

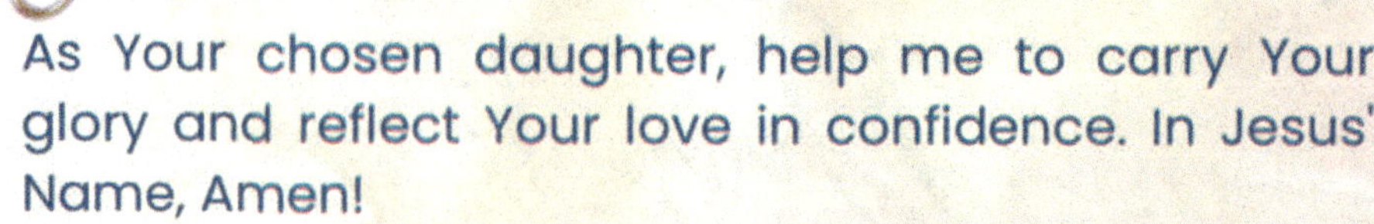

As Your chosen daughter, help me to carry Your glory and reflect Your love in confidence. In Jesus' Name, Amen!

Journal Prompt:

- Have you ever experienced a time in life when you felt unworthy or overlooked? How did it affect you?

WHO AM I?

"I am not overlooked! I am chosen, loved, and handpicked by the One who created me!

Day 2:

"God's Masterpiece"

"For we are God's masterpiece. He has created us anew in Christ Jesus, so we can do the good things He planned for us long ago." ***Ephesians 2:10 (NLT)***

A masterpiece is a beautiful work of art created with intention, skill, and creativity. It is not rushed or thrown together; instead, it is designed with patience, precision, purpose, and love.

Sis, you are not a mistake, a misfit, or an afterthought. You are God's intentional creation. Before your existence, He thought deeply about you. Your smile, your strength, your personality, and even your scars carry purpose. Every detail of your life reflects His craftsmanship. Because you are His masterpiece, you possess immense value, worth, and a unique assignment. Your life has meaning beyond comparison and competition, which makes you truly "one of a kind." You were crafted on purpose, for a purpose.

Remember, you are God's art, His beloved creation, and your existence is a beautiful testament to His beauty and power! Embrace it fully and let it shine in everything you do!

Prayer Declaration:

Dear God, thank you for creating me with skill, intention, and creativity. Remind me that I am Your beautiful work of art, unique and different. Help me to see myself through Your eyes always. I release the lies of comparison, competition, and insecurity as I embrace the beauty You placed within me. In Jesus' Name, Amen!

Journal Prompt:

- ***"Think Uniqueness:"*** What are four unique qualities God gave you that reflect His creativity? How can you embrace them more fully today?

WHO AM I?

"I am God's masterpiece, a beautiful work of art. I am intentionally created and purposed for His glory!"

Day 3:

"A New Creation"

"Therefore, if anyone is in Christ, the new creation has come. The old has gone, the new is here!"
2 Corinthians 5:17 (NIV)

Have you ever found yourself in a place where you felt stuck? Exhausted by old patterns, cycles, habits, and mistakes? The enemy seeks to keep you tied to who you **used** to be, but remember that Christ has made you new. When you surrendered your life to Him, all your old self, habits, and labels were left behind.

Sis, let me encourage you: you don't have to live in the shadows of guilt, regret, or toxic relationships any longer. In Christ, your identity is not defined by your past; it is shaped by the incredible future He has planned for you. You can walk boldly in your new identity as a beloved daughter of God! Embrace your freedom, and let His love guide you toward the abundant life He promises!

Prayer Declaration:

Dear Lord, thank You for making me new in You. Help me let go of my past life, thoughts, and regrets. I cancel every illegal voiceof the enemy, and I declare according to 2 Corinthians 5:17, in You I am a new,

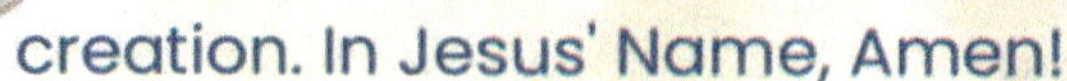

creation. In Jesus' Name, Amen!

Journal Prompt:

- What old labels, patterns, or habits have you outgrown, but still feel tied to?
- How can you begin to walk boldly in the truth that you are new in Christ?

WHO AM I?

"I am no longer who I used to be! I am a new creation; fully loved and fully free in Christ!"

Day 4:

"Crowned With Glory"

"You have made them a little lower than the angels and crowned them with glory and honor." ***Psalm 8:5 (NIV)***

Sis, God has placed a crown on your life. Not a crown of shame or defeat, but one of "glory and honor." This means you carry dignity, worth, and divine identity in Jesus, which cannot be taken away by people, circumstances, or past mistakes. Too often, we allow the world's lies to steal our confidence, but God says you are royalty and chosen to walk with authority and grace. A crown is not something you earn, but it is a gift given because you belong to Him. Wear it boldly! Wear it confidently! Even when life feels heavy, remember your crown is secure, and your worth is unshakable in Christ!

Prayer Declaration:
Dear God, thank you for the crown You placed on my life, a crown of glory and honor. Please help me to embrace my crown with confidence and humility, even when the world tries to convince me otherwise. Help me to walk in my true identity in You. Strengthen me to live in confidence as Your daughter. In Jesus' Name, Amen!

Crown Reflection Activity:

Take a few moments to reflect on what makes you crowned with *glory and honor...*

Step 1:

Draw a crown on a blank sheet of paper. Inside the crown, write words or phrases that describe your identity in Christ. (ex, crowned, chosen, loved, redeemed... etc).

As you write, remind yourself that these are not just words; they are God's truths about you. When the enemy tries to knock off your crown with lies of rejection, shame, or insecurity, come back to this drawing as a reminder: "I am crowned with glory and honor!"

Step 2:

Hang it somewhere visible (on your mirror, wall, vision board, etc.) as a beautiful reminder that your identity is not rooted in the world, but in "The Word."

WHO AM I?

"I am crowned with glory and honor. I am God's royal daughter: chosen, called, valued, and set apart for divine purpose!"

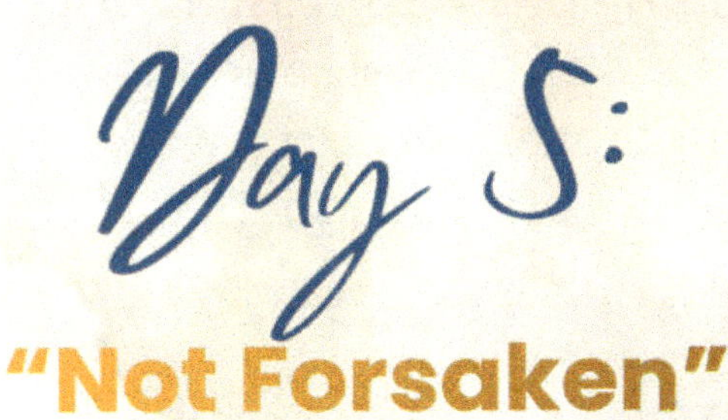

"Not Forsaken"

"The Lord Himself goes before you and will be with you; He will never leave you nor forsake you. Do not be afraid; do not be discouraged." ***Deuteronomy 31:8 (NIV)***

Have you ever felt alone, rejected, or even forgotten? Friendships fade, people walk away, doors close, and your heart may feel abandoned.

In the midst of this spirit of rejection, God offers a promise that never fails: **He will never forsake you**! He goes before you, guiding you through every step of life. Sis, because He is with you, you possess the strength, courage, and confidence to move forward. No matter who has left or what you've lost, remember that the Lord remains constant.

Hold fast to this truth: the God who leads you is the same God who never leaves you! Let His unwavering presence be your anchor as you navigate through life's challenges. You are never alone; you are always cherished and supported by Him!

Prayer Declaration:

Dear God, thank You for Your unfailing presence in my life. Even when I may feel alone, remind me that

You are near. Help me to trust Your promise that I am never forsaken, never abandoned, and never alone. Strengthen me to walk in complete confidence knowing You go before me. In Jesus' Name, Amen!

Journal Prompt:

- Write about a time when you felt overlooked, abandoned, or forgotten. How Deuteronomy 31:8 encourage you to trust that God is with you, even in that moment?

WHO AM I?

"I am not forsaken! I am not abandoned! I am not forgotten! God goes before me, walks with me, and surrounds me with His love!"

Day 6:

"Free from People Pleasing"

"Am I saying this now to win the approval of people or God? Am I trying to please people? If I were still trying to please people, I would not be Christ's servant. ***Galatians 1:10 (GW)***

"People pleasing" can feel like a heavy burden. It keeps us bound to the opinions of others, always striving to be accepted or validated. The very truth is, no matter how much we try, we will never satisfy everyone. But the good news is, we don't have to!

As a daughter of the King, your worth does not come from applause, approval, or recognition from others; it comes from Jesus. The Apostle Paul reminds us that if our mission is to please people, we miss the freedom of serving Christ fully. When we release the need for others' approval, we create space to walk boldly in the God-given purpose designed for us. True freedom is found in saying, "Lord, I live to please You alone."

Prayer Declaration:

Dear Lord, free me from the weight of pleasing people. Remind me that I am forever accepted, approved, loved, and chosen by You.

Give me the boldness to live for Your approval and not the approval of man. Help me to walk in my identity and purpose in You fully. In Jesus' Name, Amen!

Reflection Prompt:

- Make a list of the people, places, or situations where you've felt pressured to seek approval from them instead of God. Take a moment to reflect: What fears or expectations kept you bound?

WHO AM I?

"I am free from the burden of pleasing people! My identity and worth are secured in Christ alone!"

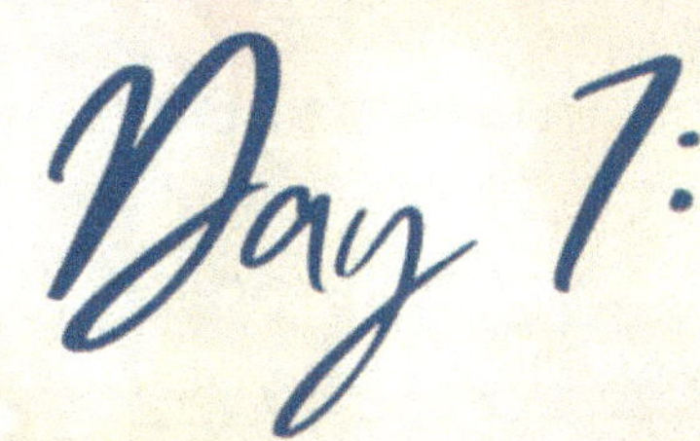

Day 7:

"Reflection & Renewal– A Prayer Walk"

"Be still and know that I am God." **Psalm 46:10 (ESV)**

You have journeyed through powerful truths these past six days discovering your worth, newness in Christ, your royal identity, and the freedom to stop pleasing people. Now, it's time to pause and reflect deeply on all that God has revealed about who you are.

A prayer walk offers you an opportunity to quiet your mind, listen to God's voice, and invite His presence to renew your spirit. As you walk, whether outdoors or in a quiet space, meditate on these affirmations: **I Am Chosen! I Am Made New! I Am Crowned with Glory! I Am Not Forsaken! I Am Free to Stop People-Pleasing!**

Let each step be a reminder of your identity in Christ, allowing His truths to sink deep into your heart. This is your moment to embrace the beauty of who you are and the purpose he has for your life!

Prayer Walk Instructions:

1. Find a quiet place to walk or sit comfortably.
2. Take slow, deep breaths and focus on God's

presence.

3. Reflect on each truth from Days 1-6. Speak each truth quietly or out loud.
4. Ask God to help you internalize these truths and release anything still holding you back.
5. End your walk by thanking God for the transformation happening in your life.

Journal Prompt:

- What truth from these first six days has impacted you the most?
- What do you feel God is asking you to release or embrace as you move forward?

Week 2:

Royalty & Worth (Living as Daughters of the King)

Last week, you began the journey of rediscovering who you are in Christ: chosen, crowned, and never alone. You faced the lies about your identity and started reclaiming the truth that you are God's masterpiece.

As we enter Week 2, it is time to step into your "royalty and worth!" This week is all about learning to walk like the daughter of the King you already are not striving to earn love but standing confidently in it. Being a daughter of the King means you carry heavenly value, divine authority, and unshakable dignity. Remember, your past does not define your worth, your mistakes, or anyone's opinions. Your worth was settled at the cross.

This week invites you to lift your head high, adjust your crown, and live from a place of beloved confidence and boldness. Let God remind you that royalty is not just a title but a transformation. You have been crowned with His grace and called to represent His Kingdom on earth.

This week's focus: Royalty! Worth! Kingdom Authority! Embrace these truths and let them transform how you see yourself and how you move through the world!

Day 8:

"A Royal Priesthood"

"But you are a chosen people, a royal priesthood, a holy nation, God's special possession, that you may declare the praises of Him who called you out of darkness into His wonderful light." **1 Peter 2:9 (NIV)**

Sis, you were never meant to blend in; you were born to stand out. You are a royal priesthood, not because of a status or title, but because God says you are. You are His daughter, chosen and set apart to represent His Kingdom on earth. As part of a royal priesthood, you carry both authority and access – the authority to speak God's truth and the access to enter His presence freely.

Remember, you belong in divine spaces, not because of perfection, but because of purpose. Even if you didn't grow up surrounded by luxury or favor, God still says you are "royal" because you belong to Him. So sis, lift your head, adjust your crown, and walk boldly in your royal calling!

Prayer Declaration:

Dear God, thank you for choosing me to be a royal priesthood and crowning me as a queen. Help me to walk boldly in whom you designed me to be, carrying the power and influence you have given me.

When I doubt my place, remind me that I belong to you, the King of Kings. Continue to strengthen my confidence and humility as I walk in my royal identity and purpose. In Jesus' Name, Amen.

Activity – Step into Your Crown:

Take a few moments to write down the areas in your life where you have been thinking or acting beneath your royal identity. Beside each area, write a truth that reminds you who you are in Christ.

Example:

- Insecurity—"I "am fearfully and wonderfully made."
- Fear – "I walk in power, love, and a sound mind."

TRUTHS TO DECLARE:

"I am a royal priesthood, chosen, anointed, and crowned with purpose. I walk boldly as a daughter of the King!"

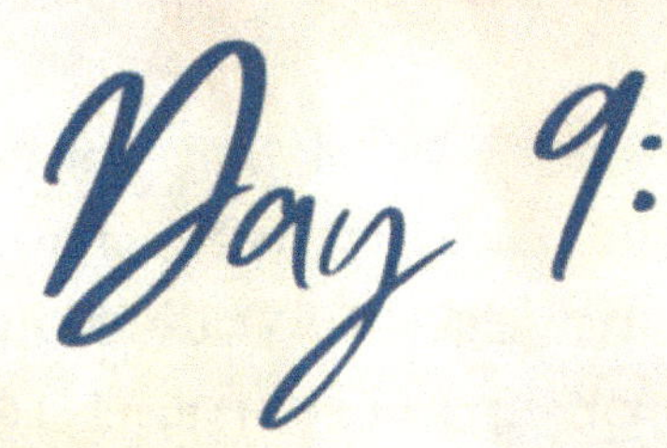

"Seated In Heavenly Places"

"And He raised us up with Christ and gave us a seat with Him in the heavens. He did this for those in Christ Jesus." **Ephesians 2:6 (NCV)**

Sis, have you ever felt small, overlooked, or beneath your purpose? It is easy to forget your true position in Christ when life gets hard, battles get tougher, or people don't recognize your value. But Ephesians 2:6 reminds us that **you are already seated with Christ in heavenly places**.

This means you carry authority, favor, and access to God's promises. You are not stuck on the sidelines of your own life; you are in the throne room with the King. Your struggles or circumstances do not define your status; your identity in Him does.

Walking in this truth changes your mindset. You stop shrinking, doubting, or settling. You begin to live **confidently, boldly, and royally**, knowing you belong in the divine spaces God has prepared for you. Even when the world overlooks you, your seat with Christ is secure!

Prayer Declaration:

Dear Heavenly Father, Thank You for seating me with Christ in heavenly places. Help me to live in the authority, favor, and identity You've given me. When I feel overlooked or small, remind me of my true position as Your daughter. Teach me to walk boldly, confidently, and royally in every area of my life. In Jesus' Name, Amen.

Journal Prompt:

- How can you begin living today as someone seated in heavenly places with Christ?
- Are there areas where you are still feeling "below your calling?"

TRUTHS TO DECLARE:

"I am seated with Christ in heavenly places. I walk in authority, favor, and confidence as a daughter of the King!"

Day 10:

"Daughter, Not Slave!"

"Now we are no longer living like slaves under the law, but we enjoy being God's very own sons and daughters! And because we're His, we can access everything our Father has –for we are heirs because of what God has done!" ***Galatians 4:7 (TPT)***

You are not bound by fear, performance, or the need to prove your worth; you are a daughter of the Most High King. Through Christ, you have been adopted into God's royal family, granted full access to His presence, love, and inheritance. An enslaved person works to earn approval, but a daughter rests in the assurance of already being accepted. You do not have to chase validation or bear the burden of others' opinions. God's love is not conditional; it is a covenant.

Sis, as His daughter, you walk in freedom, grace, and true identity. So lift your head high and remember that you are not forgotten, rejected, or unworthy. You are loved, seen, and chosen. You don't have to beg for a seat at the table your Father has already saved you a place! Embrace that truth and letit empower you to live boldly in your royal identity.

Prayer Declaration:

Father, thank You for calling me Your daughter. Help me to break free from every mindset that makes me feel unworthy of Your love. Teach me to rest in who I am in You, fully accepted, deeply loved, and chosen to inherit Your promises, in Jesus' Name, Amen.

Activity: From Chains to Crowns

On a separate piece of paper, draw a line down the middle of the page. On one side, list the '*slave mindsets'* you have carried *(ex, fear, shame, guilt, striving for approval).* On the other side, write '*daughter truths*' that replace each *(ex, loved, accepted, free, chosen, royal*). Hang this sheet of paper on your mirror or place it in a safe place where you can discover it.

TRUTHS TO DECLARE:

"I am not a slave to fear, shame, or guilt! I am a daughter of God, free, chosen, and heir to His promises!"

Day 11:

"Clothed in Strength & Dignity"

"She is clothed with strength and dignity; she can laugh at the days to come" **Psalm 31:25 (NIV)**

When God clothes you, He doesn't dress you in your past, your insecurities, or your weaknesses. He wraps you in strength and dignity. Strength is not about never feeling weak; it's about standing firm in who you are when life tries to strip you of your confidence. Dignity is knowing your worth even when others don't recognise it. Together, they create a holy covering that reminds you: **you are not defined by what you've lost or by what others say, you are defined by whom God says you are.** When you walk in this truth, you can face the future with peace and laughter, knowing that no matter what comes, your identity is secure in Him.

Prayer Declaration:

Dear Heavenly Father, Thank you for clothing me in strength and dignity. When I feel weak, remind me that Your strength is my covering. When the world tries to strip away my worth, remind me that I am already clothed in Your righteousness and grace.

Help me to walk boldly and gracefully, reflecting the beauty of a woman rooted in You. Teach me to laugh without fear of the future because my confidence is not in circumstances, but in Christ, who holds my future securely.

Today, I put on the garments You've prepared for me: faith, courage, peace, and joy. May I carry myself as the royal daughter You've called me to be, in Jesus' Name, Amen.

Journal Prompt:

- What areas of your life do you need to be "reclothed" in God's strength and dignity? Write them down and ask the Lord to renew how you see yourself in those areas.

___

___

___

___

___

___

___

___

___

TRUTHS TO DECLARE:

"I am clothed in God's strength and dignity. My worth is secure, my future is safe, and I walk boldly in whom He created me to be!"

Day 12:

"Crowned With Authority"

"Look, I have given you authority over all the power of the enemy, and you can walk among snakes and scorpions and crush them. Nothing will injure you."
Luke 10:19 (NLT)

As a daughter of the King, you carry divine authority. This authority is not rooted in arrogance or pride; it embodies spiritual confidence. Jesus has already bestowed upon you authority over the enemy, fear, and anything that seeks to rob you of your peace. Too often, we live below our God-given power, shrinking back as if we are helpless. But Heaven has already declared your victory!

Having authority means you can speak to the storm and command peace. You can resist temptation and walk in freedom. You can stand boldly, knowing that God backs your words. Remember, you do not fight for victory; you fight from victory! Embrace this truth and step into the power that is rightfully yours as a beloved daughter of the King. Live boldly and confidently, for you have been equipped to overcome!

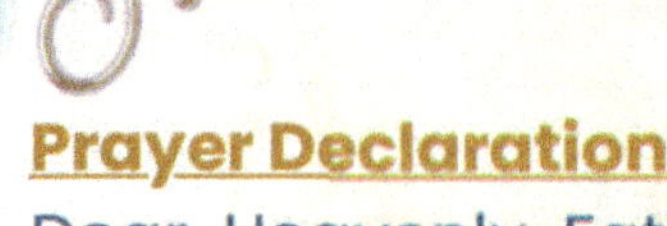

Prayer Declaration:

Dear Heavenly Father, thank You for the authority You have given me through Christ. I no longer walk in fear or defeat because You have given me power to overcome every plan of the enemy. I declare that I am clothed in Your strength, armed with Your Word, and protected by Your Spirit. Every serpent and scorpion that tries to rise against me is already under my feet. I walk boldly in Kingdom authority, not by my own might, but by the power of Jesus Christ who lives in me. I am more than a conqueror, and I reign with confidence as Your daughter, in Jesus' Name, Amen.

Reflection Activity: Mirror of Authority

Find a mirror and stand in front of it. Look yourself in the eyes not with doubt, but with confidence in who God says you are. Speak these truths aloud:

- **"I have authority through Christ!"**
- **"I am not defeated. I am victorious!"**
- **"The power of God lives in me!"**
- **"I am bold, fearless, and equipped for every battle!"**

As you declare each truth, notice how your posture shifts. Straighten your shoulders. Lift your head. You are not walking as a victim; you are walking as a **victorious daughter of the King.**

- Then, write in your journal how this reflection made you feel. Did you sense more confidence? Peace? Determination?
- Let this moment remind you that your authority in Christ is not based on emotion; it is based on **identity!**

TRUTHS TO DECLARE:

"I walk in divine authority. I am not powerless. I am a daughter of the King, equipped and empowered to overcome every scheme of the enemy!"

Day 13:

"Crowned For Kingdom Purpose"

"Your kingdom come, Your will be done, on earth as it is in heaven." **Matthew 6:10 (ESV)**

Sis, you were not only crowned to look royal; you were crowned to reign with purpose. Every daughter of the King carries a heavenly assignment here on earth. God did not choose you by accident. He placed you in this generation, this family, and this city on purpose. Your crown represents authority, the responsibility to reflect God's glory, speak His truth, and carry His love wherever you go. Sis, do not shrink back or question your placement. Remember, you are Heaven's representative on earth, crowned for Kingdom work!

Prayer Declaration:

Dear God, thank You for crowning me with purpose and placing me where I can shine for You. Please help me to see every space I enter as a kingdom assignment. Grant me boldness and confidence to walk in authority and grace to reflect Your love in Jesus' Name, Amen.

Journal Prompt:

- Where has God positioned you right now to make a Kingdom impact? In your home, workplace, or community? How can you represent His Kingdom there?

TRUTHS TO DECLARE:

"I am crowned for kingdom purpose—chosen, appointed, and sent to make Heaven known on earth!"

Day 14:

"Reflection—Walking in Royalty"

"And has made us kings and priests unto God and His Father; to Him be glory and dominion forever and ever." ***Revelation 1:6 (ERV)***

You have spent the past days discovering your identity: chosen, crowned, renewed, and seated with Christ. Sis, now it's time to walk it out. Riches or titles do not define royalty; it's about your posture! It is reflected in how you carry yourself, the life you speak into existence, and your responses in faith, even when life feels heavy.

As a daughter of the King, you are set apart, full of purpose, and clothed in grace. Royal living means aligning your thoughts, actions, and attitude with Heaven's perspective. Remember, when you walk in royalty, you represent God's Kingdom wherever you go! Embrace your royal identity and let it shine through every aspect of your life. You have the power to impact the world around you with the love and truth of Christ!

Prayer Declaration:

Father, thank You for reminding me that I am royalty in You. Please help me to walk with the confidence, grace, and humility of a true daughter of the King. May my life reflect Your glory and draw others to Your Kingdom. I choose to live as who You say I am—crowned, chosen, and confident in You. Amen.

Reflection Activity:

Take a few quiet moments to reflect on the first two weeks of this devotion.

- What truth has transformed the way you see yourself?
- Where have you noticed growth in your confidence or mindset?
- What areas still need renewal or surrender?

Then, write a short declaration or prayer committing to walk boldly in your royal identity.

TRUTHS TO DECLARE:

"I walk in divine royalty, confident, covered, and called for God's glory!"

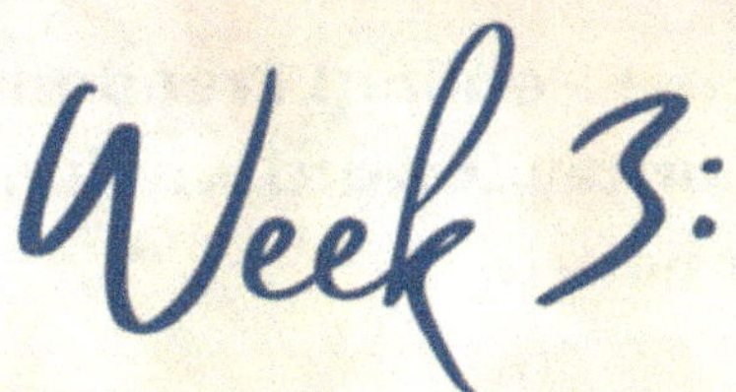

Healing & Freedom (Restoring the Broken Places)

As we embrace this powerful transition from identity and royalty, we now step into a sacred space: the realm of inner healing and restoration.

You have spent the past two weeks discovering who you are in Christ: chosen, crowned, royal, and worthy. However, before you can fully walk in that identity, God wants to touch those parts of your heart that still carry pain, disappointment, or fear. Healing is not a sign of weakness; it is *transformation*—the moment when your heart catches up to what Heaven already knows about you.

This week, I encourage you to open your heart to the gentle work of the Holy Spirit. Allow Him to reveal the hidden wounds that still need His healing touch, trusting that He will meet you with compassion, not condemnation.

You are not too broken to be healed. You are not too far gone to be restored. The same God who crowned you with glory now desires to make you whole.

This week's focus: Healing! Freedom! Restoration! Embrace this journey toward wholeness and let His love mend your heart.

Day 15:

"He Heals the Brokenhearted"

"He heals the brokenhearted and binds up their wounds." ***Psalm 147:3 (NIV)***

There was a time in my life when my heart felt shattered, a space where loneliness and hopelessness surrounded me. During my season of being emotionally and physically bullied, I struggled to understand how God could create something whole from what felt so broken. But even in that place of pain, He was near. God did not rush my healing; He gently met me in my brokenness and began restoring what I thought was lost forever—my identity!

When we face heartbreak or sadness, whether through bullying, betrayal, or disappointment, God promises to bind up the wounds of our souls. His healing is not merely about feeling better; it is about being made new. He doesn't just patch us up; He transforms our pain into purpose and our scars into stories of His grace.

Let today remind you: your brokenness is not the end of your story; it is the very place where God begins to rebuild! Embrace the journey He has for

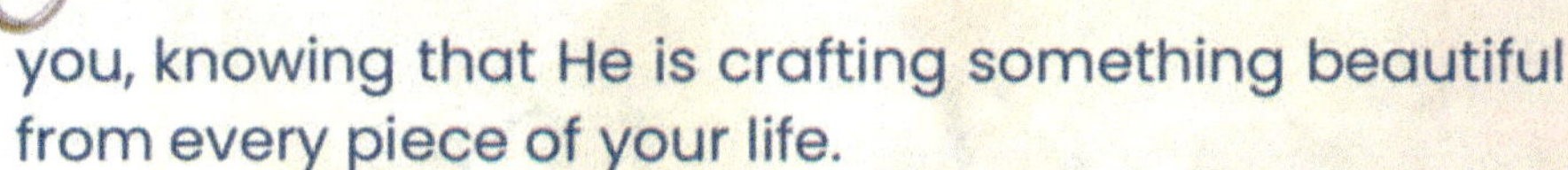

you, knowing that He is crafting something beautiful from every piece of your life.

Prayer Declaration:

Dear Lord, thank You for being near to the brokenhearted. I give you every piece of my heart that still hurts. Heal me from the inside out and help me to trust Your timing in my restoration. Thank you for turning my pain into purpose, in Jesus' name, Amen.

Journal Prompt:

- Reflect on a time when your heart felt broken. How did God begin to bring healing, even in small ways? Where might He still be mending your heart today?

HEALING CONFESSION:

"My heart is safe in God's hands. He is healing every place that has been broken, and I am being made whole again!"

Day 16:

"Beauty for Ashes"

"To all who mourn in Israel, He will give a crown of beauty for ashes..." ***Isaiah 61:3 (NLT)***

Have you ever walked through a season that left you feeling burnt out, overlooked, or broken? Life's pain can sometimes leave behind ashes, remnants of what used to be. However, God specialises in taking those ashes and turning them into something beautiful.

Sis, God does not discard your past; He redeems it. Every tear, disappointment, and heartbreak can become a testimony to His transforming power. You may have lost something, but you are not lost. God is restoring you from the inside out. Where there was mourning, He brings joy. Where there was shame, He wraps you in praise.

Remember, you are proof that beauty can rise from ashes. Embrace this truth and allow God to work in your life, creating something magnificent from the broken pieces.

Prayer Declaration:

Dear Heavenly Father, thank You for turning my ashes into beauty. When I am tempted to dwell on what has been lost or broken, remind me that You are making all things new. Help me to see Your hand

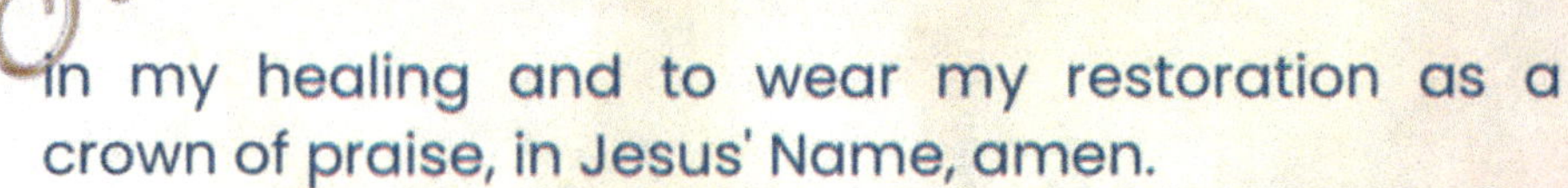

in my healing and to wear my restoration as a crown of praise, in Jesus' Name, amen.

Journal Prompt:

- What "ashes" in your life is God asking you to surrender so He can bring beauty?

HEALING CONFESSION:

"I am being restored. God is turning my pain into purpose and my ashes into beauty!"

Day 17:

"Strength In Weakness"

"But he said to me, 'My grace is sufficient for you, for my power is made perfect in weakness."
2 Corinthians 12:9 (NIV)

Weaknesses are not failures. It is an invitation. When we reach the end of ourselves, we find the beginning of God's strength. Paul discovered that his limitations became the very place where God's power could shine the brightest. The world teaches us to hide our weakness, but God asks us to bring it to Him. Every area where you feel inadequate, exhausted, or unworthy is a space for His grace to rest.

Sis, you do not have to pretend to be strong. You do not have to constantly hold it all together or be strong for everyone else. It is okay to admit when you are weary, because even in your weakest moments, God is still strong in you and for you. His strength fills the gaps you cannot. So today, instead of striving, surrender. Let your weakness become a testimony of His strength working through you!

Prayer Declaration:

Dear God, thank You for being my strength when I have none left. Teach me to rest in Your power instead of striving on my own. When I feel weak, remind me that Your grace is enough and that my weakness is not failure; it's a doorway for Your strength to shine through. Help me to release the pressure to always be strong for everyone else, and instead, trust You to hold me together. In my moments of surrender, let Your strength be made perfect in me, in Jesus' Name, Amen.

Activity — Trading Weakness for Strength

Grab a few sticky notes. On each separatesticky note, write down at least one area where you feel weak (i.e., insecurity, fear, exhaustion, etc.).

Then, stick the "weakness" notes somewhere private (like a wall or mirror). Then, as you pray, replace or cover them with "strength" truths — a visual reminder that God's grace is greater than your weakness.

HEALING CONFESSION:

"God's power is made perfect in my weakness. His grace is enough for me. Always has been and always will be!"

Day 18:

"Casting off Shame"

"Therefore, there is now no condemnation for those who are in Christ Jesus." **Romans 8:1(NIV)**

For many years, I struggled with insecurities, suffering, persecution, betrayal, and emotional bullying. I even found myself doing things I knew I should not have, which led me to confront feelings of shame. Shame became a quiet shadow that followed me, whispering lies that I was unworthy and unloved. However, when I encountered the truth of God's Word, I discovered that in Christ, there is no condemnation.

Sis, when you belong to Jesus, your past no longer holds power over you. The enemy thrives on guilt and regret, but grace silences both. The blood of Jesus has covered every sin, mistake, and wrong choice. To cast off shame means rising and remembering who you truly are: **forgiven, chosen, and free.** You are not defined by what happened to you, nor are you defined by what you have done. You are who God says you are His redeemed daughter, restored by His love. Embrace this identity and let go of anything that no longer serves you!

Prayer Declaration:

Dear Heavenly Father, thank You for setting me free from the weight of shame. For so long, I carried the pain of my past—the insecurities, betrayal, and wrong choices that made me feel unworthy. But you stepped into my story with grace. You showed me that my past mistakes do not define me; *you do.*

Lord, thank You for transforming my pain into purpose and my shame into testimony. Help me to see myself through Your eyes, forgiven, loved, and made new. When guilt or condemnation tries to return, remind me that the blood of Jesus covers me. From this day forward, I choose to walk in freedom and confidence, knowing I am fully restored in You. In Jesus' Name, Amen.

Journal Prompt:

- What situation or mistake still tries to make you feel shame? Write it down, and then beside it, write how God's grace has already redeemed that part of your story.

____

____

____

____

____

____

____

HEALING CONFESSION:

"I am not condemned. I am covered in grace, forgiven, and free from shame!"

Day 19:

"God's Peace Over My Mind"

"And the peace of God, which surpasses all understanding, will guard your hearts and your minds in Christ Jesus." ***Philippians 4:7 (ESV)***

There are moments in life when your mind feels like a battlefield, filled with worries, "what ifs," and fears of the unknown. I have been there too, when anxiety tried to control my thoughts and steal my peace. But God's Word reminds us that His peace is not something we have to earn; it is a gift He freely gives when we rest in Him.

The peace of God goes beyond logic or understanding. It does not depend on circumstances but flows from His presence. When your thoughts begin to spiral, pause and invite the Holy Spirit in. God's peace will stand guard over your mind like a shield, protecting you from fear and unrest. Sis, you do not have to figure everything out; you only need to trust the One who holds your mind, heart, and future in perfect peace.

Prayer Declaration:

Dear Heavenly Father, thank You for being my peace. When my thoughts become heavy or filled with fear, help me to surrender them to You.

Teach me to rest in Your promises and to trust that You are in control. Guard my heart and my mind with Your perfect peace. Let Your calm presence silence every anxious thought. Today, I receive the peace that surpasses all understanding in Jesus' name. Amen.

Journal Prompt:

- What thoughts or situations have been robbing you of peace lately? Write them down, then speak God's Word over them and release them into His hands.

HEALING CONFESSION:

"The peace of God guards my mind. I live in divine calmness and confidence through Christ Jesus!"

Day 20:

"Forgiven and Free"

"God is faithful and reliable. If we confess our sins, he forgives them and cleanses us from everything we've done wrong." **1 John 1:9 (GW)**

Did you know that sometimes the hardest person to forgive is "yourself"? The enemy loves to whisper reminders of your past mistakes, trying to convince you that you are still bound by shame or guilt. How do I know? Because he does the same thing to me. He will attempt to send people, places, and even situations to remind me of what God has already freed me from. However, God's Word declares that when we confess our sins, He is faithful and just to forgive and cleanse us from all unrighteousness. This means our slate is wiped clean, and our past has been forgotten completely.

You do not have to keep reliving what God has already redeemed. Forgiveness is not about forgetting; it's about freedom. You are no longer defined by what you did but by what Christ did for you. So, sis, walk in that truth today—remember that you are forgiven and free!

Embrace this new identity and let it transform how you see yourself and your past. You are a cherished daughter, deserving of the grace and freedom that come from above!

Prayer Declaration:

Dear God, thank You for forgiving me of my past completely. Please help me to release every weight of guilt and shame that tries to follow me. Even when the enemy tries to bring up my past, help me to bring every thought into the obedience of Jesus Christ. Remind me daily that I am no longer a prisoner to my past or mistakes. Thank you for your freedom, peace, and restoration, in Jesus' name, Amen.

Journal Prompt:

- What area of your life are you still carrying guilt or shame for, even after God has forgiven you? How can you begin walking in the freedom Christ already gave you?

HEALING CONFESSION:

"I am forgiven, redeemed, and free. My past no longer holds me. God's grace has set me free!"

Day 21:

"Reflection—My Healing Journey"

"The LORD is near the brokenhearted; he saves those crushed in spirit." **Psalm 34:18 (CSB)**

Healing is not always a straight path; it is a journey of surrender, forgiveness, and rediscovery. For many years, I carried the weight of low self-esteem, depression, and unforgiveness from the pain of being bullied and rejected. I smiled on the outside but was silently breaking within. Yet through it all, God was nearby. Through every tear and silent cry, He was there, gently piecing me back together.

My healing did not happen overnight. It came through prayer, letting go, and allowing God to show me who I truly am in Him, not who others said I was. Every wound became an open door for His love to flow deeper. Sis, as you reflect today, remember, healing is not about perfection; it is about progress. God is restoring your heart and renewing your mind so you can walk freely in your divine purpose.

Prayer Declaration:

Dear God, thank You for walking with me through my healing journey. Even in moments I did not feel You,

You were there comforting, restoring, and renewing me. Thank you for healing my heart and reminding me that my story still carries purpose. Help me to continue walking in freedom and peace, trusting that You are not done with me yet in Jesus' Name, Amen.

Reflection Activity:

Take time to journal or pray through the following prompts:

- In what areas have I seen God heal me since starting this devotional?

- What moments of growth, forgiveness, or freedom am I most grateful for?

- Where do I still need to invite God deeper into my healing process?

After reflecting, thank God aloud for every step of your healing, even the small ones.

HEALING CONFESSION:

"My healing is in progress, and God is with me every step of the way. My brokenness has become beauty through His love!"

Week 4:

Crowned to Reign—Fulfilling Your God-Given Purpose!

Last week, you journeyed through **healing and freedom,** allowing God to restore the broken places within you. You released pain, shame, and old identities that once held you back. Now, you are stepping into *your purpose*—fully healed, whole, and ready to reign.

Week 4 is all about embracing your God-given purpose with boldness, confidence, and faith. You were never meant to blend in; you were called to shine as *salt and light* in a dark world. God has *appointed you for fruitfulness,* equipped you with everything you need, and placed you in this generation for a divine reason. As you run your race, remember that every step of obedience brings glory to Him.

You are not walking in your own strength but in divine empowerment. The same Spirit that raised Jesus from the dead lives in you, strengthening, guiding, and positioning you for victory. As you live out your calling, keep in mind that boldness does not equate to perfection. It means trusting God enough to move forward even when you feel unqualified.

This week, you will be reminded that you are a ***Lioness in the Spirit, a Light to the World, and an Ambassador of Heaven***. You were chosen to influence, serve, and lead with grace. Your crown is not just for display; it is a call to reign with purpose! Embrace your identity, and step boldly into all that God has for you!

Day 22:

"Salt and Light"

"You are the light of the world. A town built on a hill cannot be hidden. Neither do people light a lamp and put it under a bowl. Instead, they put it on its stand, and it gives light to everyone in the house. In the same way, let your light shine before others, that they may see your good deeds and glorify your Father in heaven." ***Matthew 5:14-16 (NIV)***

As daughters of God, we are called to influence and impact the world, not to blend in but to stand out. Jesus said we are both salt and light: salt preserves, adds flavor, and heals. Light reveals, guides, and exposes darkness. When you walk in your God-given identity, you bring truth, hope, and love into every space you enter.

The enemy wants you to dim your light out of fear, insecurity, or comparison, but God placed something radiant inside of you. Your light was never meant to be hidden; it was meant to point others to Him. Do not underestimate your presence. Someone's life may be changed because you decided to shine.

Prayer Declaration

Dear Heavenly Father, thank You for calling me to be the salt of the earth and the light of the world. I declare that my light will shine brightly wherever I go, in my home, workplace, ministry, and community. I will not dim my light to fit in or please others. I am chosen to bring flavor, healing, and truth to those around me. Let my life reflect Your love and draw others to You, in Jesus' Name, Amen.

Journal Prompt:

- In what areas of your life have you hidden your light? How can you boldly shine for Christ in your family, work, ministry, or relationships this week?

DECLARATION OF FAITH:

"I am the light of the world and the salt of the earth. I will shine for God's glory!"

Day 23:

"Appointed for Fruitfulness"

"You did not choose me, but I chose you and appointed you that you should go and bear fruit, and that your fruit should remain, so that whatever you ask the Father in my name, He may give it to you." ***John 15:16 (ESV)***

Sis, you were handpicked by God, not by accident or chance, but by divine appointment. When God chose you, He did not just call you to exist; He called you to bear fruit. Fruit that remains. Your purpose is meant to produce something lasting: lives changed, hearts encouraged, and faith strengthened! However, fruit does not grow overnight. It takes pruning, patience, and staying connected to the Vine, Jesus Christ.

Sometimes it may feel like nothing is happening, but even in hidden seasons, God is cultivating something within you. Every "no," every delay, and every stretch is preparing your roots for greater fruit. Remember, you are appointed to be fruitful in every area of your life—spiritually, emotionally, and purposefully. Your fruit will speak for you!

Prayer Declaration:

Dear Lord, thank You for choosing and appointing me to bear lasting fruit. Help me stay rooted in You so that everything I produce brings glory to Your name. Even in pruning,I trust You are preparing me for greater fruitfulness. In Jesus' Name, Amen.

Journal Prompt

- What has God been cultivating in you during this season? What fruit do you believe He wants to bring forth through your life?

DECLARATION OF FAITH:

"I am chosen and appointed by God to bear lasting fruit!"

Day 24:

"Running the Race with Perseverance"

"Therefore, since we are surrounded by such a great cloud of witnesses, let us throw off everything that hinders and the sin that so easily entangles. And let us run with perseverance the race marked out for us, fixing our eyes on Jesus, the pioneer and perfecter of faith." **Hebrews 12:1-2 (NIV)**

Sis, life can feel like a race, but remember that it is "your race," uniquely marked and designed by God just for you. You don't have to compare your journey to anyone else's—their finish line is not yours!

The enemy may attempt to slow you down with distractions, doubt, or discouragement, but God calls you to keep moving forward. Let go of anything that weighs you down—past mistakes, fear, insecurity, or criticism—and run with perseverance. Fix your eyes on Jesus, the One who both begins and perfects your faith. When you run in His strength, every step counts, every moment matters, and victory is guaranteed!

Embrace the path laid out before you, and trust that God is with you every step of the way. You've got this, and the finish line is all yours!

Prayer Declaration:

Dear Heavenly Father, thank You for the race You have set before me. I choose to run with perseverance, casting off every weight, fear, and distraction. Help me fix my eyes on Jesus, trusting His timing and guidance in every step. Strengthen me to run boldly in my purpose, knowing that victory is mine because I am running in Your power. In Jesus' name, Amen.

Journal Prompt:

- What weights or distractions do you need to throw out so you can run your race with focus and perseverance?

DECLARATION OF FAITH:

"I will run my race with purpose and perseverance!"

Day 25:

"Guarding Your Crown"

"I am coming soon. Hold on to what you have, so that no one will take your crown." ***Revelation 3:11 (CSB)***

Your crown represents your identity, authority, faith, and reward in Christ. A symbol of who you are and what you have overcome. However, just like in the natural world, a crown can slip if we stop walking in alignment with God. The enemy will try to distract you, discourage you, or cause you to doubt your worth. But Jesus reminds us, "Hold on to what you have." This means to stay steadfast in faith, protect your peace, guard your purity, and stay rooted in His truth, even when life tests you.

Sis, you have come too far to let the enemy snatch what God placed on your head. Guard your crown through prayer, obedience, and discernment. Remember, you are crowned with glory and honor, and no one can take what God has ordained unless you give it away.

Prayer Declaration:

Dear Heavenly Father, thank You for the crown you have placed upon my life.

Please help me to guard it with wisdom and strength. Give me discernment to recognize distractions and courage to stand firm in faith. I refuse to allow fear, comparison, or compromise to steal what you have crowned me with. I will hold fast to my faith and walk in the victory you have already given me. In Jesus' Name, Amen.

Journal Prompt:

- What "crown" has God placed on your life in this season (i.e., peace, purpose, joy, and calling)? How can you actively guard it from distraction, doubt, or discouragement?

DECLARATION OF FAITH:

"My crown is secure because my life is anchored in Christ Jesus!"

Day 26:

"Bold As A Lioness"

"The wicked flee when no one pursues, but the righteous are bold as a lion." **Proverbs 28:1 (NIV)**

Sis, there is a holy boldness that comes from knowing who you are and whose you are. A lioness does not apologize for her roar. However, she moves with confidence, authority, and grace because she knows the power within her. In the same way, God is calling you to rise with spiritual courage and to walk boldly in your purpose. You do not have to shrink back or second-guess what He placed inside you.

Fear, doubt, and insecurity may have tried to silence you in the past, but today God is reminding you that righteousness gives you access to divine confidence. The Holy Spirit will empower you to speak truth, move in faith, and walk with authority in every space you enter. This is not arrogance; it is Kingdom confidence. **You are crowned, chosen, and commissioned to roar!**

Prayer Declaration:

Dear Lord, thank You for filling me with the boldness of a lioness.I pray You will help me to no longer shrink back or doubt what You have placed within me.

Strengthen my voice, my faith, and my confidence to walk in my divine purpose. I declare that I am fearless, courageous, and full of Your Spirit. Wherever I go, I carry the authority of Heaven within me, in Jesus' Name, amen.

Journal Prompt:

- What areas of your life have you allowed fear or insecurity to silence you? Write down one way you can take a bold step of faith this week to walk in your God-given authority.

DECLARATION OF FAITH:

"I am bold, fearless, and a lioness in the spirit. God's power roars through me!"

Day 27:

"God's Ambassador"

"So we are Christ's ambassadors; God is making his appeal through us. We speak for Christ when we plead, "Come back to God!" ***2 Corinthians 5:20 (NLT)***

Sis, you are Heaven's representative here on earth. Chosen to reflect the heart, character, and message of the King. As an ambassador of Christ, your words, actions, and presence carry influence. You do not only live for yourself, but you also live to reveal His love and truth to others.

Sometimes we forget that our daily lives, whether at home, work, or even online, are opportunities to represent the Kingdom. Being an ambassador of Christ does not mean being perfect; it means being available and surrendered. When people see you, they should see His grace, His peace, and His compassion shining through you. You are His voice of hope and His vessel of restoration in a broken world.

Prayer Declaration:
Dear Lord Jesus, thank You for trusting me to be Your ambassador. Help me walk in wisdom, humility, and love so that my life points others back to You.

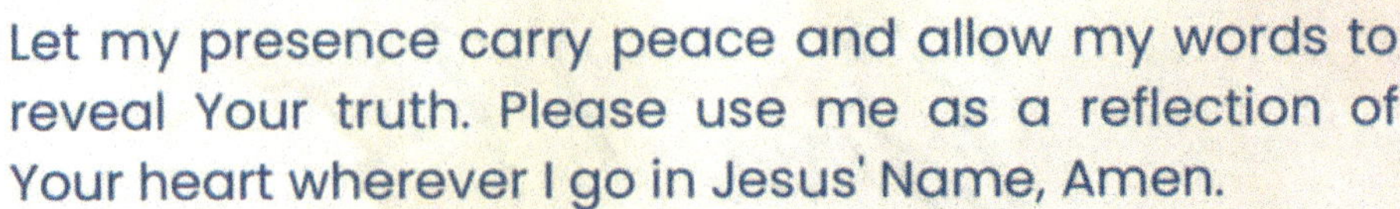

Let my presence carry peace and allow my words to reveal Your truth. Please use me as a reflection of Your heart wherever I go in Jesus' Name, Amen.

Journal Prompt:

- In what ways can you better represent Christ in your daily life? How can your words, attitude, and actions reflect His Kingdom more clearly?

DECLARATION OF FAITH:

"I am Heaven's representative on earth!"

Day 28:

Reflection—Walking My Purpose

"And who knows but that you have come to your royal position for such a time as this?" **Esther 4:14 (NIV)**

Sis, you were not placed here by accident. Every chapter of your story, the victories, the pain, and the lessons have led you to this moment. Like Esther, God has positioned you with purpose, favor, and influence to impact lives for His glory. Your identity in Christ is no longer hidden beneath fear, shame, or comparison. You are chosen, crowned, and called.

Walking in purpose does not always look glamorous. Sometimes it is found in small acts of obedience. Showing love, forgiving others, speaking truth, or simply saying "yes" when God calls. Each "yes" moves you deeper into your divine assignment. Remember, Queen, you have been prepared for such a time as this.

Prayer Declaration:

Dear God, thank You for calling and positioning me for this time. I surrender my plans and align myself with Your will.

Give me courage to walk boldly in my purpose and confidence to know that I am exactly where You want me to be. Let my life bring glory to You, in Jesus' Name, Amen.

Reflection Activity:

On a separate sheet of paper, take a quiet moment to write a letter to yourself titled *"For Such a Time as This."* In it, thank God for how far He has brought you and declare your commitment to walk boldly in your purpose. Place your letter in a safe place to revisit often.

DECLARATION OF FAITH:

"I was created and positioned for such a time as this!"

Day 29:

"Empowered To Reign"

"No, in all these things we are more than conquerors through Him who loved us." ***Romans 8:37 (NIV)***

Sis, you have been healed, restored, and equipped. Now, it is time to walk fully in the victory that Christ has already won for you. Step into your calling with confidence, knowing that every trial you faced has been preparing you for this moment. Your past does not define you, and your limitations do not restrict you. God's power flows through you, giving you the strength to overcome, influence, and impact those around you.

Walk boldly, not in arrogance, but in the assurance that you are a daughter of the King, chosen to reign in life. Your testimony, gifts, and obedience are powerful tools for His Kingdom. Today, embrace the authority, freedom, and purpose that Christ has already provided, and let your life shine brightly as a reflection of His glory. You are capable of great things—now go forth and make a difference!

Prayer Declaration:

Dear Heavenly Father, thank You for calling me to reign with you.

I thank you for every season that has shaped me, every trial that has refined me, and every moment that has drawn me closer to your heart. I receive the strength, authority, and confidence that comes through Christ. Remind me daily that I am more than a conqueror by my own power, but by Your Spirit within me.

Help me to walk boldly in my purpose, to use my influence for your glory, and to lead others to the freedom I have found in You. Today, I declare that I will no longer shrink back or doubt who I am in you. I am crowned, chosen, and empowered to reign in Jesus' Name, Amen.

Journal Prompt:

- In what areas of your life do you need to step into victory and authority? How can you actively live in the power God has given you?

____

____

____

____

____

____

____

____

DECLARATION OF FAITH:

"God empowers me to reign in every area of my life with grace, strength, and authority!"

Day 30:

"Commissioned to Reign"

"Therefore, go and make disciples of all nations....a nd surely I am with you always, to the very end of the age." ***Matthew 28:19-20 (ESV)***

Sis, you have come through 30 days of rediscovering your worth, reclaiming your identity, and walking in divine purpose. Now, this is your commissioning moment! You have been healed, restored, and reminded of your worth and identity in Christ. It is now time to go forth and reign.

Walking in purpose is not just about what you do; it is about who you become in the process. You are a vessel of God's love, a carrier of His truth, and a reflection of His Kingdom. Just as Jesus sent out His disciples, He sends you—to speak hope, to serve in love, and to live boldly in faith. Remember, sis, you do not have to walk alone. The same Spirit that empowered Christ now empowers you. So, live in Him and embrace this commissioning to reign! Step into the calling He has for you, and let your life be a testimony of His greatness!

Prayer Declaration:

Dear Heavenly Father, thank You for calling, equipping, and sending me.

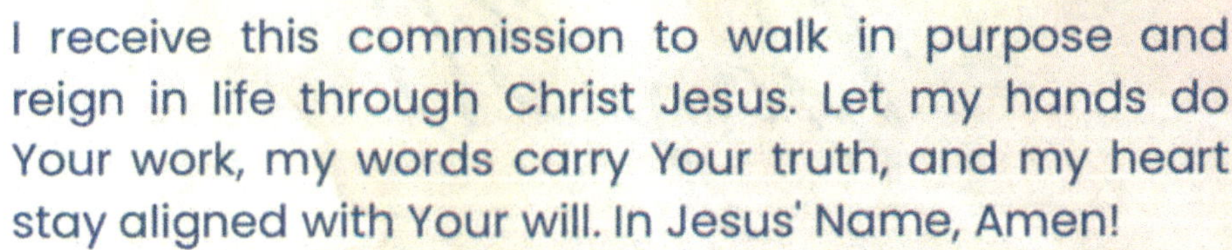

I receive this commission to walk in purpose and reign in life through Christ Jesus. Let my hands do Your work, my words carry Your truth, and my heart stay aligned with Your will. In Jesus' Name, Amen!

Reflection Activity:

- Take a quiet moment to sit before God. Write down what "reigning" looks like for you in this next season—at home, in ministry, at work, and in your personal growth. What has He called you to step into with boldness? End your reflection with a prayer of surrender and commitment to your Kingdom assignment.

___

___

___

___

___

___

___

___

___

___

___

DECLARATION OF FAITH:

"I am commissioned to reign. I walk in divine authority, grace, and wisdom.I am crowned for purpose and chosen to lead with love.I carry Heaven's power withinme, and everywhere I go, I bring light,peace, and victory.I reign with Christ now and forever!"

Meet the Author

JALICIA N. RICHARD

Jalicia N. Richard is a wife, mother, and faith-based women's empowerment leader called to help women rediscover their worth, identity, and divine purpose in Christ. With a heart for restoration and healing, Jalicia uses her testimony to remind women that their past does not define their future; God does!

For many years, she faced deep struggles with insecurities, low self-esteem, depression, and the pain of verbal, emotional, and physical bullying. But through her journey of healing and surrender, she has experienced the redeeming power of God's love and grace. Now, she boldly walks in her calling to empower other women to do the same. As the founder of a women's empowerment ministry, *"A Femininity Care,"* Jalicia imparts and ministers to the hearts of women, encouraging them to embrace their God-given identity, reign in confidence, and live from a place of divine purpose.

"Chosen to Be Crowned," a 30-day devotional journal, was birthed from her personal journey as a reminder that every woman is chosen, loved, and crowned by the King of Kings!

Special Thanks:

Jalicia is grateful for her loving husband, Alvin Richard, her family, friends, and ministry team, all of whom have supported her vision and helped bring this devotion to life. She would also like to thank every supporter who is courageous enough to embark on this beautiful journey of healing, restoration, and purpose. May God clothe you with His love and beauty always and forever!

If you would like to learn more about Jalicia and her work, you may visit her website:

www.femininitycare.com

A Prayer Over You

Dear Heavenly Father,

I thank you for this beautiful woman who has journeyed through these 30 days with you. Thank you for drawing her closer to your heart and restoring the truth of who she is in Jesus Christ. May every seed planted through these pages take root and flourish in her life. Let her walk boldly in her God-given identity: chosen, loved, crowned, and confident in whom you have called her to be.

Where there was once pain, allow your healing to manifest and overflow. Where there was confusion, bring divine clarity. Where there was shame, allow her to wear your glory as her crown. Remind her daily that she is loved, seen, and equipped for every good work.

Father, as she lives out her purpose, continue to guide her steps and breathe a new life within her. Surround her with your peace, cover her with your favor, and let her light shine brightly for your kingdom.

In Jesus' Mighty and Sweet Name,
Amen.

Made in the USA
Coppell, TX
02 February 2026

70767992R00075